The Broker Who Broke Free

The Broker Who Broke Free

MAITREYA ISHAYA

ISBN-13: 978-1484066416
ISBN-10: 1484066413

For the heroes who are willing to do whatever
it takes to be free

CONTENTS

What am I doing with my life?

A top investment bank, London. 8 a.m. November 2000.

It's Monday morning. My eyes are sunk into dark sockets, my skin is clammy and I have far too many wrinkles. I've been in the office for two hours, thinking about how much I hate my life. It is so hard to be present.

There are two phones at my desk, one for each ear. Their tangled chords remind me of yesterday's final trade. A trade where I had a screaming match with a client, whose heart had been sealed shut with molten lead. Life has become one long hangover.

Back then I knew there must be more to life, but I'll be damned if I knew what it was. I didn't even enjoy the good things anymore. I was just existing, not living.

What am I doing with my life? I thought, day after day. Yet still I did it. Still I turned up for work. An unseen force pushed me to sell my soul as a Sales Trader, in one of the hottest financial cauldrons on earth. Perhaps it was ambition? Perhaps it was fear? Perhaps I just had no idea what else I could do to make so much money?

Whatever it was, it pushed me to live a life I didn't want. I was chasing the dream of financial freedom. Yes, I was chasing the 'dream', but forgetting to enjoy life on the way. I was twenty-five years old, yet most of the time I felt like an old man, aching with the boredom which filled my so-called successful life.

But my unhappiness had less to do with my job than I realized back then. If I'd only been able to take a step back, I would have seen that the job itself wasn't that bad. In fact, some of my colleagues loved it. But I couldn't step back. I was too involved, my head full of thoughts which pulled me in different directions.

Quit.
Don't quit.
The money's too good—just hang in there for a few years.

Nothing's worth this pain, not even the cash.

But it didn't suit me. I thought I could do anything if the money was good enough, but that wasn't true. Chatter, chatter, chatter, my mind was so chaotic that I didn't realize I needed to give up chasing the dollar, discover my life's purpose, and follow that.

That was over a decade ago, and now my life is very different. I was a bit hesitant to tell my story. Yet, fate led me from the trading floor through a series of adventures, and I emerged with a tale to tell which might just inspire you.

This book is short, because writing about freedom is nothing in comparison to directly experiencing it for yourself. This book's purpose is to let you know, that it *is* possible to be free from your mind—to move beyond worries and mental pain, and to be at peace with yourself and the world, no matter how your life looks. Perhaps this is something you already know, and perhaps it sounds too good to be true, but the fact that you are reading shows that you are open to the possibility. Then, if you decide to take up the gauntlet and do something about finding peace, well, that's entirely your choice.

Earning a crust

I left university with a degree in zoology but I had no intention of working with animals. After three years of peering at them through microscopes and cutting the poor blighters into little pieces, I'd had enough. Instead, I got a job building horse jumps. I guess that could be called working with animals, but I didn't sit on a horse once and only patted them occasionally. Horses made me very nervous.

I worked with some great people, and I loved being outdoors. We used whatever we could lay our hands on to build impressive jumps. I got to use chainsaws, hammer nails, drive trucks, eat a lot of junk food, and live in an old caravan. It was pretty much heaven on earth for a young guy with no responsibilities who'd been brought up in the countryside.

I travelled around Britain getting paid to do something I enjoyed, surrounded by friends, going to parties, and having a great time. Sometimes I lived in a smelly old caravan, and sometimes I stayed in the wings of grand, stately homes which were so huge I could have got lost in them. They say that variety is the spice of life, and there was plenty of it.

Many of the horse riders I met were an inspiration. They galloped across the countryside, throwing themselves and their huge beasts over jumps which could kill lesser riders. They never knew if they were going to make it home in one piece! Yet still they did it. These were people who lived for the moment, and it was great to be around them.

To this day, that simple, menial job was one of the most satisfying things I've done. But I wasn't meant to continue with it. Back then I wasn't someone who was easily satisfied. Since I was very small, I knew there was something I was meant to do with my life, but I had no idea what it was. I had a feeling I'd been born with a purpose and that I wouldn't be happy until I'd fulfilled it. This feeling made me restless and kept me searching for something better, always on the lookout for a greener patch of grass. So, it was inevitable I'd look for something else to do.

One morning I woke up in the caravan, which smelt worse than ever. The windows were fogged up and covered in green mould, and I didn't dare open the fridge for fear of what might be living in it. It was winter in the north of Scotland. The electric heater was broken, and I was bloody freezing. I'd been thinking about my future for a few weeks. Yes, I enjoyed the freedom of building jumps, but it wasn't a job for someone who wanted to make an impact in life. I needed to get a proper job, with prestige, prospects, and money, a job which people would respect me for. I started to dream up a cunning plan. If I could become an equities broker, make loads of money, and buy a nice place in Thailand …

Well, who wouldn't be happy living in a tropical paradise?

That day I quit my job.

Dick Whittington

A few weeks later, I packed a bag and moved to London. It was good to be out of the caravan. Although I missed my friends, I knew it was time to embark upon a new adventure. It was also time to make some serious cash.

At that time the economy was booming. So it didn´t take me long to get a temping job in the 'back office' of an American bank in the Docklands. It wasn't a glamorous position, but it was a foot in the door, a chance to learn something about finance. It was also a formidable boost to my CV.

The Docklands was still a relatively new development, and to call the area sterile would have been paying it a great compliment. All steel and concrete, with very little charm, Canary Wharf felt like a cross between a graveyard and a doctor's waiting room. And the excitement of the job matched the charm of the area. The back office turned out to be more tedious than I could have imagined. I was basically a human computer, but without the talent for maths. My job entailed checking for possible errors on trades and sitting at my desk for hours on end, pretending I was busy when I wasn't.

The American work ethic was to work hard and play hard, so anyone who was seen as lazy didn't last long. At a time when Facebook was just a glint in Mark Zuckerberg's eye, there was little to distract me from the boredom. If there was no work to do, rather than grab a coffee and have a chat, I was compelled to stay at my desk and look busy. As you can imagine, much of my day consisted of daydreaming as I hunched over my computer pretending to work. It was all about pretending—pretending to work, pretending to be interested, pretending that everything was okay. I started to miss my caravan.

Luckily, at school I'd mastered the well-known technique of nodding with a serious expression on my face whenever I was presented with a boring situation. Whenever a teacher talked to me about something I had no interest in, I just furrowed my brow and nodded, it seemed to keep them happy. The nodding technique proved invaluable at work, and after a few months there was even talk of a promotion. I wasn't keen on taking another boring job, though. I had bigger fish to fry. I wanted to get to the 'front office', also known as the trading floor as soon as possible.

In my mind the trading floor was the Holy Grail—a chaotic, dangerous place where billions of dollars were thrown around and fortunes were made and lost every day.

Although, I'd never met one in the flesh, I was convinced that the traders were the real men. They were the ones who made the money, the ones who got the hottest women. Confident and impressive, they lived life on the edge. Like lions they ruled the jungle, and everyone knew it.

I also knew I had it in me to be the best sales trader ever. After all, I'd seen the movie *Wall Street* enough times, to know I was one of those lions. Yes, I was a lion…

Alas, this pussycat didn't realize he was in for a nasty surprise.

After a year, I had enough work experience to convince my future employers that I had an undying commitment to capitalism and was willing to put myself through hell on earth to be rich. It was time to muscle my way onto the trading floor.

Interviewing for positions in the most

powerful investment banks on earth was a rush. I loved it. Every time I put on my pinstriped suit, straightened my tie, and pushed my way through the glass doors of some ludicrously wealthy financial institution, I felt indestructible. It was like stepping into a world which few people dared enter.

The traders who interviewed me were impressive and driven. I loved the feeling of importance this world gave me. I was moving into the realm of the movers and shakers. They were the people who made things happen. They were the ones who had real power, perhaps even more power than the politicians because they controlled the money *and* didn't have to answer to voters. I was soon going to get a whiff of that power. Back then that meant I was becoming a *somebody*. I mattered, or so I thought. It was like a drug to me, and I made sure I was going to get my fix.

Job interviews are strange things. I was never 100 percent sure what they were looking for, but I figured that schmoozing the interviewer without being caught schmoozing was the way to go. Maintaining the fine balance between saying the right thing and not looking like an arse-kisser was something I prided myself in.

'What are your weaknesses?' some Maserati-driving big shot would ask me.

'I'm a perfectionist, and I tend to work too hard', I'd reply with a furrowed brow, once again using the nodding technique to great effect.

Or I'd say, 'Sometimes I just give too much and get exhausted.'

They must have heard those lines a thousand times, but perhaps they recognized that this cocky twenty-three-year-old could make them money. I guess that was what the interviews were really about: working out if the candidate could make money for the bank and, more importantly, boost their own bonuses.

My ethics, morals, and beliefs seemed irrelevant in these interviews. No one ever asked me if I felt it was important to be honest or to have integrity, and frankly I didn't care about either quality. It was no place for do-gooders or bleeding hearts—it was the City of London. People were only useful when they were making money.

The nodding technique continued to help me tremendously, and I was offered a few places on some fast-track graduate training schemes. One in particular stood out because it included a six and a half thousand pound bonus just for taking the job *and* a two-month, all-expenses-paid training course in New York.

Dazzled by this new world, I was sucked into the lure of big money and quickly forgot about the things which had been so important to me: helping people, having fun, and making the world a better place.

The new me cared far more about my pay cheque than my happiness. So, with dollar bills in my eyes, I signed on the dotted line and was enrolled as a sales trader in one of the biggest financial machines on earth.

The Trading Floor

As the girl at the desk handed me an identity badge, I couldn't help smiling to myself. As far as I was concerned, I had arrived. I was twenty-four years old and about to embark on an adventure which would give me all the things a young man, with no clue about life, thinks matter: fast cars, nice houses, and sex appeal. And even better, I was heading off to New York for a two-month training stint. Ready to take a huge bite out of the Big Apple.

My employers were going to put me up in a lovely hotel on Manhattan Island and educate me in the ways of equities trading. I was going to learn how to be a Gordon Gekko, right in the heart of the Big Apple, *and* they were going to pay me for it!

Had I been a bit older and wiser, I might

have realized that in the finance world, you don't get something for nothing. But I was blissfully unaware of this, and within a few days I was living it up in New York. Being wined and dined in famous restaurants, hanging out in trendy bars with the other trainees, and enjoying sumptuous breakfasts at the local diner. It was another taste of heaven. If only I hadn't had to pass the wretched exams that they set us. But even those were not so bad, and somehow I scraped through.

All too quickly my training was over, and I was heading back to London to repay the favour my bosses had done for me—with blood, sweat, and tears.

Working as a sales trader was surreal to say the least. My office was right in the centre of London, close to St. Paul's Cathedral. The contrast between the modern glass structure and the ancient church couldn't have been greater. That area of London was bustling with life. It was where the old City met the new City. Old money met new money, and an obscene amount of both was on display. Cool bars and shops lined the streets, and it was hard to count how many supercars passed by every hour. The old buildings reminded me that this part of the world had been a financial powerhouse for a very long time. I remember it as a place which was bigger than the people in it, a place with a history rich in tradition, innovation, and greed. It was a place where you either won big or went home with your tail between your legs.

My office had over three hundred people in it. It was an enormous, open-plan office with nowhere to hide. You could have mistaken it for a semiconductor factory. There was not even a solitary pot plant to remind us that Mother Nature existed. And unless you had a desk near one of the windows, you might not see the sun all day. My desk was right in the middle.

As a junior, I'd be one of the first people into work in the morning. They say money doesn't sleep, and my co-workers seemed to live by these words. If I was in the office at six in the morning, I was never alone. The room was full by 7 a.m.

To my surprise, most of what I'd been taught in New York wasn't going to help me become a good sales trader. I had learnt a lot of theory, statistics, and economic philosophy. But if I was going to make it in this business, I needed more. The best traders were the guys who were good with people, men and women who built relationships, talked their way out of tricky situations, and kept the right people happy at the right time. It could be a fun job if you were good at it, with a lot of laughs. It could also be hellish, depending on your approach to the whole thing. Mental strength and enjoying the job were vital to survive.

I called my clients every day and gave them my ideas on what the market was going to do. I told them which shares were hot and if I had any bright ideas which would turn their millions to billions. If they liked my ideas, they'd give me their business, and if they didn't like them, or me, they wouldn't even answer my calls. Most of them knew far more about the market than I did, and this scared the hell out of me. They were the experts, and I was just a trainee. It was a dog-eat-dog world, and all the dogs were smarter than me.

In this game, information was money. Some of that information came from our screens, some from our phones, and some from listening to each other's conversations. It was impossible to take in everything which happened around me. But the more info I could filter, the more useful I was to my clients. I constantly felt under pressure to be on top of what was going on.

At my desk I had six computer screens in front of me. There were TVs hanging from the ceiling over my head, blasting out all the bad news which CNN and Fox could find that early in the day. Porsche car keys littered the desks around me, left in full view as a not-so-subtle reminder of what was most important here.

Quite quickly, I honed the ability to do many things at once. I could type an email while talking to a client on the phone and half listening to a conversation next to me. This multitasking may not sound that impressive to the ladies reading this book, but for a man to focus on more than one thing at a time was considered a great talent!

The days varied from fast and furious to deadly calm. I was at my best when it was busy, even though I moaned about it. The quiet times, which became more frequent as the markets slowed down, were funereal. Everyone knew that if the slump which hit us in the late nineties kept going, it was only a matter of time before heads rolled and bonuses vanished into thin air.

From time to time, the markets turned the wrong way, or someone made a mistake or broke a promise. Those were the times when I'd find out if I was fit for the job or not. To my utter dismay, I wasn't as fit as I'd hoped. I remember on more than one occasion buying a stock instead of selling and watching the figures plummet. Running across the floor, my heart in my mouth, I barged through my colleagues to try to rectify my mistake. I had the deal reversed, and within seconds I'd lost a quarter of a million dollars. Back at my desk, I sat with my head in my hands, feeling like the bottom had just dropped out of my world.

Then a voice came over my intercom; it was a senior trader. 'You screwed that one up, you stupid idiot.' Now, if I'd been a good sales trader, I would have taken it on the chin, apologized, and got on with it. Instead, I fumed for a couple of minutes and then marched over to the senior trader, who was sitting at his desk.

'What the hell is your problem? I'm just a new guy, and I screwed up. There's no need to rub my nose in it', I spat.

He turned his head towards me and stood up. It was only then I realized I was picking a fight with the biggest guy on the floor. At almost six foot six, he towered over me. Images of David and Goliath would have flashed before me if I hadn´t been so scared and angry.

'Trainees shouldn't speak to their betters like that', he said in a cool voice.

Again, if I'd been a good sales trader, I would have backed down and offered to buy him a drink. 'You dickhead, there's no need to be like that. I screwed up. I'm sorry, okay?' My words were apologetic, but my tone told him I was so angry that I might do something really stupid if he pushed me further.

Luckily, he was the wiser man and backed down. Actually, he turned out to be quite nice. He offered to buy me a drink, which showed me one reason he was a senior trader and I wasn't. I was extremely lucky that time, but I also felt a sneaking fear that I couldn't handle the stress of the job.

Traders spent all day, five days a week, on the trading floor. If we didn't enjoy the work, we were heading for trouble. If I'd been honest with myself, I would have seen that I didn't really enjoy the job after the excitement of the first few weeks had passed.

As you can imagine, there were a lot of characters in that world. There were the super-serious business graduates, who lived and died for their work. They didn't take lunch. They didn't smile and spoke in a calm monotone which could send me to sleep in seconds. A quick sandwich at their desks was enough to power these cyborgs for the day. Shutting out all emotion, they just pushed ahead no matter what. Like sinister Andromedans they could and would do anything to make a buck, if the end justified the means. What they lacked in charisma they made up for in knowledge and Ivy League educations. They seemed to be a necessary evil in the bank, and so good at making money that their lack of social skills was overlooked. They scared the hell out of me.

At the other end of the spectrum were the barrow boys. The East-end geezers, who'd worked their way up from nothing, shouted a lot and managed to have a good laugh most of the time. They spurned the American work ethic and took a lot of boozy lunches with their clients. They relied on their charm to get them what they wanted. I really liked those guys.

I can't tell you the name of the bank I worked for, as I had to sign a gagging order. This was presumably to stop me from bringing them into disrepute with slanderous tales of insider dealing and sexual harassment. Truth be known, I don't have any juicy stories of insider dealing. And I never heard of anyone being pressured into sleeping with the boss in return for a promotion. It may have happened, though.

The most dramatic incident I saw was when a big equities trader threw a colleague (who happened to be his best friend) across a desk and smashed his face into a computer screen. It all happened in a flash. The trader exploded over some deal which had cost him money, grabbed his friend, and the next moment he was airborne. But the pair of them were soon friends again, drinking together in the pub later that day. It was that kind of place: high tempo, high octane, high stress.

Wrong place, wrong time

As my time as a trader stretched from weeks into months, I became more and more discontented with work. My previous excitement for the job was replaced by a feeling of doubt which gnawed away at me. I suspected I was in the wrong place, doing the wrong thing, and at the wrong time. I wanted to enjoy work, but I couldn't seem to shake the feeling that I was supposed to be doing something else with my life—something significant, but I didn't know what. Even my scooter rides into London had lost their appeal, as I became less and less present, my mind preoccupied with problems and doubts.

Every weekday morning, I would jump on my bright red chariot and ride into work. When I first started working in London, those scooter rides were one of the highlights of my week. I just loved the feeling of being on that 125 cc racing machine. It was so easy to forget my troubles, and to be present with the sights and sounds of London. My mind disengaging from the worries of life, and a sense of freedom replacing the incessant thinking that I usually experienced. I would drive over Battersea Bridge, along the Thames, past the Houses of Parliament and Big Ben, and into the old City. I used to love carving my Piaggio Sfera through the almost empty roads.

But now when I drove into work, I no longer had that feeling of freedom. I was no longer just on the back of my bike. In my mind, I was somewhere else. I was already at work, planning what I was going to do that day, figuring out how I was going to schmooze my clients, or just arguing with my colleagues in my head.

I'm embarrassed to write that I often lost those imaginary arguments and insisted on playing them over and over in my head until I won. Sometimes it took me a few attempts, but in the end I always prevailed. I prided myself on always winning them. I think I needed to get out more!

I didn't notice the beauty of the ride anymore, and I didn't appreciate the tight turns. I was so distracted, it was a miracle I ever made it to work in one piece.

When I finally got to there, I should have been present with what I was doing. But instead I started daydreaming about what I was going to do after work.

Where shall I go out?

What's the name of that great restaurant?

Will the cute girl from HR be there?

I should have been giving much more attention to my job. Exciting things happened every day. News from somewhere around the world would come in and immediately effect the stockmarket, sometimes causing huge falls or rises in share prices. The market was so alive and sensitive to what was going on in the world, it could have been a very exciting place to be. But it was hard for me to enjoy it when I wasn't actually there. My thoughts took my attention away from what was happening. I was rarely present.

When I left work each day—you guessed it—I wasn't present then either. I was busy reviewing what had happened that day. Or I was planning the next day. I was addicted to thinking. I was so addicted that I couldn't stop, even when I wanted to. Most of the time, my body was in one place and I was somewhere else, and it sucked. Looking back, I find it strange, yet I had no idea then it could be any other way. My addiction to thinking was the root of many of my problems, dare I say *all* my problems. But what could I do? I had no idea how to stop.

The pressure which had been so exhilarating when I first started to trade now sat as a tight knot in my stomach. The long days sitting in front of computers took their toll. I wanted to quit, but I didn't.

Every week the pressure mounted. Getting out of bed in the morning became more difficult. Looking at myself in the bathroom mirror became more disheartening. The thoughts in my head kept on battering me.

God, you look terrible.

Look at those wrinkles—you're getting old.

So, why did I stick at it? Why not just quit? Put it all down to experience and move on?

Well, I was terrified of missing out on what I thought was my only chance to be happy. But fate's noose was tightening around my neck, pushing me to realize that being happy was not about the perfect future. I was being forced to see that happiness is about how you are right now. By living for tomorrow, I was actually getting more and more unhappy today.

Crumbling plans

My 'retire to a beach in Thailand' plan had initially seemed so brilliant. Yet with hindsight it had much in common with Baldrick in Blackadder´s ingenious plans. Just like Baldrick I displayed an unwavering optimism and belief in what I was doing, and did not even consider that it might end in failure. At the time it had seemed like a no brainer. I´d work hard for ten years, rake in an obscene amount of cash and then take it easy for the rest of my life. This plan was what got me up at five in the morning, when all I wanted to do was go back to sleep. Wasn't hanging out on the white beaches of Ko Samui worth working my butt off for? But who was I kidding?

I knew I wasn't following my heart, but even worse, I didn't know *how* to follow it. I didn't know how to be happy. Deep down I had a feeling there was so much more to being a human than I was experiencing. And that bugged the hell out of me.

But what could I do? I remember lying in bed, staring at the blackness behind my eyelids as I waited to fall asleep. I really wanted to sleep, but there was so much going on in my mind that I couldn´t. Planning, analyzing, regretting what I'd done, fantasizing about the future: my mind never seemed to stop. I wanted happiness, and this job was my one shot at it. My greatest dream had become my greatest burden.

Some people's life-changing stories are brave and heroic. You must have heard a few of them. Against the odds, an ordinary person musters up great reserves of internal courage, takes a huge risk, and it all pays off in the end. You get the picture.

I, on the other hand, wasn't even remotely heroic. I'd wanted to leave my job for a year and a half but still hadn't thrown in the towel. Instead of quitting I just moaned a lot.

In those days, I bored my brother Charlie and my friends by telling them my story over and over again. They all told me, 'Just quit. Your happiness is much more important than a job.'

But the words didn't sink in. Looking back, I'm amazed anyone wanted to spend any time with me at all. And as time went on, fewer did.

Then one day, by chance I found an old photo of me on my first day working in London, dressed in a suit and with a big smile across my face. I squinted at the photo, hardly recognizing the vibrant guy in it. Taking it to the bathroom mirror, I held it next to my reflection. It was a huge shock. My once healthy face looked drawn. I'd lost weight, and the sparkle in my eyes was gone. I needed some time off work. So, later that week, I walked into the doctor's surgery with a good sob story already prepared.

'Hmm. Well, I need to make sure you really need sick leave. Orders from above, I'm afraid.' The doctor spoke without looking up from his papers. I took a deep breath, ready to give him an Oscar winning performance that would have made the hardest heart melt in sympathy for my plight.

'So what job do you do? '

'I'm a trader in the city,' I replied, ready to recite my story.

'Two or three weeks?' he asked, without batting an eyelid.

Hurray! For the next three weeks, I was a free man. I flew up to my parents' home in

Scotland to get some perspective. With their help it didn't take long to see the wood from the trees.

I decided to quit. It was tough to admit it to myself, after I'd invested so much energy in the prestige, the money, and my Christmas bonus, but life was too precious to waste doing something which I didn´t enjoy.

It felt as if a lead weight had been lifted from my shoulders. Free at last! If I could have done a backflip, I would have.

Humbled by life

Fittingly, it was pissing down with rain when I took the train to work for the last time. As I passed the looming structure of Battersea Power Station, I remember feeling nervous and hoping that I was doing the right thing. My mind was busier than usual, churning on thoughts about my decision to pack the job in.

Do I really want to quit?

Am I ready to throw away an opportunity that many people never get?

Just another couple of years, surely I can do that.

Nope, I'm quitting, it's already decided.

Fortunately my mobile woke me from my thoughts. It was my dad, and he sounded even happier than usual.

'Ollie it's Daddy here', he said, his voice booming. 'Have you seen the FT this morning?'

'No.' *The Financial Times* was the last thing I was going to read that day.

'Well, your bank is offering voluntary redundancy to all their staff. If you hold off for a week or two, they'll pay you to leave.'

'Really? Are you sure?' I asked, not wanting to get too excited.

'Yes, it says so in the paper. So it's not such a good idea to resign today.'

I couldn't believe my ears. As soon as the train had pulled into Clapham High Street, I jogged to a news-stand and bought the last *Financial Times* I've ever purchased. It was true. Today certainly wasn't the day to go into the office and resign. So I went out for a slap-up meal with a friend instead. Food had never tasted better.

A week later, I signed a piece of paper promising never to darken my bank's doors ever again. In return they gave me twenty thousand quid.

Once again, I felt on top of the world. I lived in London, doing whatever I liked, and celebrated the fact that I didn't have to go to work anymore. But slowly the feeling that something was wrong clawed its way back into my life. I still wasn't happy, and I was no closer to my goal. Perhaps I was even further away from happiness because I was no longer getting healthy pay cheques every month.

Though the title of this book might imply that I found happiness by quitting a job which didn't suit me, and casting off my responsibilities, nothing could be further from the truth. After a few weeks of feeling a tremendous sense of relief, I found myself back where I'd begun—restless, bored, and living a life with little meaning or purpose. Strangely for me at the time, the trading job had far less influence on my happiness than I'd thought.

So once again I needed to figure out what to do with my life. Dejected, vulnerable, and lost, I went for a stroll on Wimbledon Common. With a Sony Discman plugged into my ears, I tried to find inspiration in fine music. At the time I had a penchant for Westlife which few of my friends understood. The Irish crooners were just what I needed to get me into a suitably melancholic mood.

It didn't take long for the boy band's dulcet tones to set me off. And as the tears flowed down my cheeks, I hoped I wouldn't bump into anyone I knew.

Why is this happening to me? Why aren't I happy? I've always tried to be a nice person. I don't know what to do with my life. Have you ever felt like that? Have you ever felt really lost? As if you were meant to be doing something with your life, but you didn't know what it was? Have you ever felt the kind of loneliness which never leaves, even when you're amongst friends?

I'd always believed in God, which was quite surprising considering that as a child growing up in the north of Scotland, I'd been subjected to the fire-and-brimstone sermons of my rather overenthusiastic minister, a bitter man called Canon Hammock. I still retained images of that red-faced minister, preaching damnation and hellfire for all non-believers from the safety of his pulpit, and scaring the hell out of the lost souls foolish or naive enough to sit in front of him every Sunday. Hammock's sermons should have put me right off the idea of God, and kept me bound in fear of damnation forever.

But despite being threatened with an eternity in hell, I never believed him. It's interesting how kids can sniff out an idiot well before most adults can. I knew that if there was a God, he or she was probably very nice, someone who watched over me like a protective mother. So, as I trudged my way across the common, walking in time to the beat of one of Westlife's more touching tracks, wiping the tears from my eyes, I prayed.

Please help me. My life isn't working. I want to be happy. Please show me what to do.

Please!

Whenever the shit hit the fan, I always said a prayer. But this prayer was a little different. Not only was it accompanied by Queen of my Heart, but for the first time in a while, I was humble. I needed help because I was lost—completely lost—and I knew it. The cocky young guy who thought he knew it all had disappeared for a while. This was a cry for help from the bottom of my heart.

Help comes in mysterious ways

Four days later, I found myself in the hands of a shiatsu healer in Edinburgh. He was sticking his thumbs into different parts of my body, making me squeal like a stuck pig. He was a middle-aged guy, thick set, and with a heavy Scottish accent and a moustache. When I think about it now, he looked more like a policeman than a therapist.

Throughout the treatment, he was talking about some kind of meditation he did. I was vaguely open to hearing about meditation, but he was a little too enthusiastic for me. All I wanted was a massage, not a lecture on inner peace. I didn't say much, but still he didn´t take the hint and continued to share his enthusiasm for his practice like an overexcited evangelist.

I didn't understand most of what he said. He used lots of spiritual terms like 'the big self', 'the little self', 'enlightenment', 'chakras', and a whole bunch of other things which to this day sound rather strange to me. But one of the things he said piqued my curiosity.

'If you learn Ascension, it will give you more peace and joy, and it will make your life easier.'

I didn't see it at the time, but he was offering me a gift. My prayer from only days before was being answered. If only I'd been receptive enough to see it.

Despite being a clever and open guy (ahem), I didn't follow his advice. Instead, I shook his hand, told him I'd look into this meditation business, and left. I had no intention of doing any such thing.

But somewhere inside myself, I knew that the meditation thing he'd been prattling on about might actually be something for me. But I had other things to do with my life than sit cross-legged for hours on end trying to silence my mind. So my life continued very much as before, with me banging my head against a wall, whingeing and moaning about wanting to be happy but doing bugger all about it.

I was consumed with my problems and disillusioned with life, society, and the world. All I wanted was to be free from my worries, but I couldn't see a way out. Luckily, this world is a much friendlier place than I appreciated at the time. Even if I was too stupid to do anything about it, life was going to hammer me and hammer me and hammer me until I did.

Mountain rescue

A couple of weeks later, I spent a few days in the mountains of Snowdonia in Wales with a friend of mine called Mark. Mark had an uncanny ability to sniff out adventure and make light of life whenever it got a bit serious. The life and soul of the party, he was one of those guys who made people laugh, and I loved to be around him. We'd been friends since university.

I, in my inherently deluded way, liked to think that I was a good navigator. Yet as with so many things back then, my incompetence was matched only by the depth of my delusion. Quite honestly I could have got lost in a paper bag if I wasn't careful.

Mark and I decided to do some hillwalking in Wales to blow away the cobwebs and get some time in nature. Like sensible young men, we set out wearing shorts and T-shirts, and carrying a bag of crisps, a bottle of water, a button compass, and an unlaminated map. It was the middle of June, the thermometer was pushing twenty-five degrees, and there wasn't a cloud in the sky. What could possibly go wrong?

About three hours into our hike, things were going well. It was still a glorious, sunny day, and we were having a great time talking, philosophizing, and enjoying the fresh mountain air.

At midday I remember walking along a ridge when I turned around to say something to Mark, who was trekking behind me. As I was about to open my mouth, I saw something behind him which took the wind right out of my sails.

Oh shit.

On the horizon, just behind Mark's head, was a line of angry storm clouds, which were rolling towards us at a furious rate. So much for it being mid-June: I'd never seen such an ominous sky. It was like a scene from a science fiction movie, with the sky turning blacker by the minute, twisted and distorted by a force which had our number on it. Although the clouds were still a few miles away, they were blowing towards us fast, and it wouldn't be long before we were in big trouble.

Mark's terrified expression said it all. We had to get off the mountain before the storm came, and we decided we had only two choices. We could retrace our steps and clamber down the steep side we'd already hiked up. Or we could try to find our way down an apparently easier slope to our left, which would take us further away from our car but quickly to the safety of low-lying land.

Retracing our steps would take us right back to the car but meant heading straight into the storm and making a slippery descent of a few hundred metres in the wet. The second choice was more of a mystery, but with our expert map-reading skills, we were sure we'd make it down before the worst of the storm hit. What we didn't appreciate was that the slope to our left was littered with cliffs, and if we didn't get our navigation exactly right, we'd need a rope and harness to get down. We had neither.

Then the wind blew up, and it started to rain. It started with a few splatters but very quickly became a steady downpour. Mark and I both looked at each other, neither of us wanting to be the one who made the final decision. When you are caught between the devil and the deep blue sea, which do you choose?

'Let's toss a coin', I suggested.

Two minutes later we were heading

towards the slope to our left, hoping for the best.

It was strange how quickly the temperature dropped. On those mountains it can go from a balmy twenty to freezing in a matter of minutes. If we'd had a decent compass, we might have been okay. But our button compass was the kind of thing you won in a cheap Christmas cracker, so we couldn't take any reliable bearings from it. If we'd had sleeping bags, or even just good, warm clothes, we probably would have been fine.

I started to have that horrible feeling of foreboding in the pit of my stomach, the kind of feeling which comes with losing control. Every time we found a route which looked as if it would take us down to safety, we hit cliffs that we couldn't get past. We'd turn around and hike back up the hill, hoping for a better route to appear fifty metres along the mountain. We did this again and again and again, each time hitting a wall of stone which dropped into oblivion below us.

Then the fog came in. It was so dense that we couldn't even tell how high the cliffs were because we couldn't see the ground below us. Our map was soaked through and became impossible to read. The few clothes we were wearing were now drenched. Our stylish beachwear offered no warmth at all, and our easygoing smiles were a distant memory. Bright yellow Bermuda shorts may have a certain appeal in the surf, but now that they were soaked through, they were like damp sponges, sucking the cold into our skin. As our bodies started to freeze, our conversation died down to terrified silence.

Both of us exchanged concerned looks from time to time, but neither of us wanted to admit how scared we were. Mark in particular was starting to get very cold indeed. His head went down and his walking slowed as the initial stages of exposure started to set in. Both of us knew enough about the mountains to know we didn't know enough about *these* mountains to turn this thing around. We'd got ourselves into a situation way out of our depth and were paying the price for our stupidity, courtesy of the harsh Welsh elements. We were learning that Snowdonia could be a cruel and humbling place.

I remember passing an old wooden bothy. Half of the roof had collapsed, but it offered some shelter from the wind.

'We can stay in there until the weather gets better', I suggested.

'No way', said Mark. 'If I stop now, I won't start again. If we don't get off this mountain in the next hour or two we'll freeze to death—bothy, or no bothy.'

With those words, coming from a man who found it easy to make light of most disasters, the seriousness of our situation hit me hard. Then the hail came in. Pellets of ice battered us from the heavens, and we really started to freeze. I kept hoping the fog would lift, as it usually did whenever the wind came in. But this was not to be.

As the minutes passed, our plight was getting steadily worse. The colder we got, the greater our desperation to get off the mountain. The storm wasn't passing; if anything it was getting worse. If we couldn't somehow find a way back to the valley and the car, we'd die of exposure.

Usually, I could figure my way out of any mess I got myself into, but today there was no solution. There was nothing we could do except keep going and try to ignore the terror. I was so scared. Perhaps a route down would appear, but perhaps it wouldn't.

I looked to Mark for some kind of reassurance but could see he was thinking the same thoughts I was. We tried to encourage each other, but both of us were screaming on the inside, doing a poor job of quelling our rising panic. On the mountain that day, I felt so small, like a pawn in a game I couldn't control. The tears started flowing, and I didn't even bother to hide them. I only had one option left. Can you guess what I did?

Yup, you got it. I prayed. I prayed as hard as I could.

Please God, get me out of this. I don't want to die. I'll do something good with my life. I'll help people. Just get us off this mountain alive.

Surely it was not my destiny to die of exposure on a mountain. And not in Wales of all places!

Then, just a minute or two after I started praying, something happened. Something quite magical. If you're a highly logical skeptic who doesn't believe in magic, you could call it coincidence, but to this day I call it a miracle. Out of the fog appeared a group of climbers: seven men and women dressed in waterproofs, with rucksacks on their backs. They had hiking boots and all the professional kit we should have had. They were proper climbers, not just jokers like us. Yet they were no ordinary climbers—they turned out to be a mountain rescue team on a training exercise!

Can you believe it? We hadn't seen another soul all day and then, in our darkest hour, we met a group of trained mountain experts. I looked into the heavens—well, at least as far as the fog would let me—and uttered a thank you.

My jubilation contrasted sharply with

the mountain rescue team's disapproving looks. They'd seen it before: young guys without proper equipment who showed no common sense or respect for nature, cocky guys who underestimated the elements and paid the price for their ignorance.

'You were awfully lucky you bumped into us', one of them told me through gritted teeth.

He was right. Mark and I must have apologized all the way down the mountain. They made the descent which had been impossible for us look so simple, and in twenty minutes we were down. After a quick check over, they found that Mark was suffering from mild hypothermia and I was just very cold.

As we made our way back to the car, heads hanging and teeth chattering, it was my pride which hurt more than anything. I'd warm up in a hot bath, eat some steak, and probably feel myself again within a few hours. We'd been so stupid, so arrogant, but the shock had at least put things into perspective for me. If I'd died up there on the mountain, would I have been happy with the life I'd led so far? Would I have been able to look the angels at the pearly gates in the eye and say, 'Yes, I lived my life to its fullest'?

The answer was no. I'd done my best

throughout my life, but I was sure there was more to being a human than I'd discovered so far. I was sure I hadn't completed whatever mission I was meant to carry out. I wasn't going to forget my promise. It was time for me to find peace, and rise beyond the chaos which followed me around. I'd probably even book myself in for that meditation course I'd been told about. That would be a start, anyway.

Sharks

When I was safely back in London, I soon forgot my heartfelt promise on the mountainside. My humility vanished as quickly as it had arrived, and life once again overtook my intentions. Looking back, I was certainly not the brightest button in the box. But fate wasn't going to let me slither my way out of this one: if I wasn't going to do what I was supposed to do with my life, then I'd keep getting reminders. They'd keep arriving, even if they nearly killed me.

A few weeks after my mountain adventure, I drove to the south coast with some friends to spend a week in a holiday cottage near Padstow. We had a great time hanging out, enjoying pub lunches, and catching up with each other's news. And then there was the morning swim across the bay I planned to take with John and Jim.

I wonder how many millions of seaside holidaymakers regret seeing the movie *Jaws*? I certainly did. Whenever I swam in water more than three feet deep, a haunting voice at the back of my mind warned me of an imminent shark attack. Images of the movie flashed into my mind, and it seemed a gruesome inevitability that a giant fish would swallow me whole. Or, if I wasn't as lucky, it would take a leg or an arm and leave me to bleed to death. I did my best to quell the fear, but it was always there, hovering, waiting to strike if I gave it half a chance.

Another voice tried to reassure me that I was just getting carried away by my imagination. *Jaws* was just a movie; great whites sharks didn't feed off the coast of England. It was far too cold. I would be okay. I just had an overactive imagination—that was all.

On the first day, I gave the bay swim a go. It was a big swim for me, probably a couple of kilometres. But it was an adventure so why not?

In fact, I quite enjoyed it. Although it was bloody freezing when I first went in, it didn't take long to warm up, or at least for my body to numb to such a degree that I couldn't feel the cold. As long as I stayed close to my mates, I managed to keep my fear of sharks at bay and avoid freezing to death in the murky waters. Besides, getting back to the cottage, sitting in front of the warm fire wrapped in a towel, and drinking hot chocolate made up for the discomfort. Day two went pretty much the same way, and my confidence was building.

Then, on the third day, things went a little pear shaped. That day the sky was overcast and the temperature had dropped to an uncomfortable fifteen degrees. As I left the cottage wearing nothing but a T-shirt and my swimming trunks, I wondered why I was even bothering to go swimming.

'Come on, it's not that bad. Don't be such a baby', my friends sensitively reassured me. As was so often the case, I succumbed to peer pressure and went anyway.

Picking my way across the sharp barnacles which had welded themselves to the rocks along the shore, I cursed myself for giving in. I could have gone back to bed and had nothing to do with these foolish antics. Why was I always so weak?

My doubts continued as I lowered myself into the freezing water, but my friends didn't seem to care about the cold. They kept teasing me, but I pretended I was immune to their words.

The anticipation of an event is usually

far worse than the event itself. By the time we were a few hundred metres from shore, I'd forgotten about the sharks and the cold. The whole experience was actually quite pleasant.

Then, when I least expected it, John casually said, 'You know they've had shark attacks around here. People have actually been eaten off the coast of Cornwall. I hope there aren´t any hungry sharks around now, they tend to pick out the weakest swimmers.' When he said the words 'weakest swimmers' he looked straight at me.

Footage from *Jaws* suddenly appeared in my mind, and a primeval fear swallowed my guts. Despite three years of studying marine biology courses at university, knowing that the chances of being eaten by a shark were fewer than the chances of meeting Elvis in the supermarket, I freaked out.

'Screw this, I'm going in', I said, already paddling for the shore.

John and Jim just watched, unsure of whether I meant what I said or was just playing along with their joke.

'Just chill out!' John shouted after me. 'There aren't any man-eating sharks off the coast of Cornwall. We were just having a laugh.'

But I wasn't having any of it. My composure took off as quickly as a hungry greyhound out of the traps. And as if I had a bit between my teeth, I headed towards the shore, as fast as my not-so-impressive swim strokes could carry me. My arms flailed, my legs went bananas, and I started to inhale water. Then, as is so often the case whenever I panic, everything got an awful lot worse.

The wind picked up, and the waves got bigger. Seawater started to splash into my face. My eyes stung, and I panicked even more. What could have been a simple swim for shore became a nightmare. I spluttered and choked on salt water. Of course, the more I panicked, the harder it got. Fear may or may not focus the mind, but it certainly doesn't improve your swim stroke. My body tensed up, and my breath quickened. I must have resembled a stray cat which had been thrown into a cold bath as I did anything to get out of the water, no matter how desperate or stupid it was. I decided to swim to the closest part of the shore, straight into the current.

A wise man would have taken his time, swimming at an angle to the tide and keeping his cool. But I was no wise man. I was a stray cat, determined to escape from the great white shark circling below me—a shark which was bigger than any previously recorded in history, hadn't eaten for days, and happened to have a penchant for small Scottish guys.

If I hadn't had so much salt water in my eyes, I would have sworn I could see the predatory shadow closing in on me. I could almost feel the beast emerging from the depths to munch on me. I flailed my way to shore as best I could, with my friends following behind me, no doubt astonished by what was happening.

Cough. Splutter. Choke.

Swallowing salt water isn't pleasant at the best of times. But for a weak swimmer two hundred metres from shore who'd convinced himself that the tide was now taking him out to sea, it was murder. Once again, I was in trouble, out of control and at the mercy of the elements. Once again, I got humble. Of course, as was now my habit, I started to pray, just as I had on the Welsh mountainside.

"Please, just get me out this. Get me out alive, and I'll do something good with my life."

After what seemed like an hour but was probably only ten minutes, I clawed my way up the barnacled rocks on the shore. Furious with my friends for getting me into such a state, I stomped back to the cottage and ignored them for the rest of the day. I counted my blessings that I was still in one piece—no thanks to them.

Despite calling this my second brush with death, I was never really close to drowning. I'd swallowed some seawater and panicked, but that was about it. Yet in my head, I really thought I might drown, and that was the significant part for me. It's not so much what happens to us in life but how we interpret it that matters. In my mind I'd been close to death once again, so my promise was as sincere as it could have been.

Viva España

Even this second disaster didn't shake me up enough, and once more I quickly forgot my promise. My life continued very much as before. As I said, I wasn't the sharpest tack in the box.

By this stage you might be asking yourself, *Is this guy a bit slow? Is he missing a few slates from his roof? Surely he must have got the hint by now?* Well, I regret to say that common sense had never been my specialty. It was more natural to me to go blundering through life without thinking about the consequences of my actions.

The next place where I'd be sticking my head in the sand to avoid what I was really meant to be doing with my life was Spain. Once again, I had another cunning plan. I thought it would be fun to go to the Costa del

Sol and pick up a bit of the lingo. After all, half the world speaks Spanish, so I thought I might as well learn. Now, if you knew how my Norwegian sounds after living in Oslo for eight years, you'd know that I needed whatever help I could get. I signed myself up for a language course and took a cheap flight to Spain.

I lived with a rather miserable Spanish family, a few hundred yards from the beach in Málaga. The beach was pleasant enough, and I met some nice people there. But inside I still felt empty. I had transformed my outside world again, but I felt no different. The voices in my mind still found something wrong with my life. I didn't feel any closer to peace. My success with the language was even less impressive. I missed at least half my lessons and avoided my sinister Spanish family like the plague. Choosing instead to hang out with the English-speaking foreigners most of the time. All in all, I was treading water but very slowly sinking.

One evening, a few of us from the language school were enjoying a bit of local cuisine in a fish restaurant by the sea. We were speaking English, of course. At the same time, some local lads were tearing up and down the seafront, pulling wheelies and doing tricks on their scooters, trying to impress whatever girls were around. I laughed sarcastically as they fell off their bikes, picked themselves up, and kept going, oblivious to how ridiculous they looked. In that part of Spain, it seemed very much the norm to humiliate yourself in the most dramatic way possible to impress the ladies. I guess the subtleties of courtship vary across the globe!

A little later, we headed home, after filling ourselves with local paella and a few San Miguels. I was with a friend of mine, a girl called Kim. As we walked along the beach, three of the scooter guys appeared out of nowhere and started revving their engines. They were clearly attempting to impress Kim, who happened to be a very attractive American.

If you haven't had the pleasure of seeing someone rev a 50cc scooter engine in an attempt to win the heart of an intelligent young woman, I strongly recommend it! It was hilarious. Had I not felt so hostile towards these men, I would have collapsed with the giggles. Unsurprisingly, Kim wasn't that impressed. But her lack of interest seemed to excite the lads even more. They continued to squeeze as much noise from their two-wheeled lawnmowers as they could.

Clearly intrigued by this alluring foreigner who wouldn't succumb to their charms, they got off their bikes and decided to try a more traditional method, chatting her up. Despite their best efforts to invade Kim's personal space, looking her up and down and making strange whistling sounds, they still failed to impress her. Can you believe it?

I kept quiet, hoping they'd go away. After all, the locals could be quite enthusiastic with their courtship rituals, and they probably didn't mean any harm. However, the leader of the gang kept hassling her and wouldn't take no for an answer. I was in one of those uncomfortable situations where I hoped everything would sort itself out but feared I might have to do something brave.

As the scooter guys continued to bug Kim, I knew that enough was enough. These macho idiots were getting annoying. A split second before I opened my mouth, I saw myself saying in a calm and commanding voice, 'Leave it out, guys, she's not interested.'

But in those days, diplomacy wasn't a talent of mine, and slightly different words came out of my mouth:
'Piss off, you dickhead, she's not interested.'

Of course, in the spirit of living in Spain, I said it in Spanish—or rather, I tried to say it in Spanish. What actually came out of my mouth could have been anything. But at least one of the guys understood the 'piss off' part of my sentence, and his face hardened.

I've never been a tough guy, but at times I used to think I was. Without further ado, I moved towards him, my body tense and ready for the impending violence. The prospect of fighting this good-for-nothing scoundrel to save a damsel in distress was drawing closer. I was confident I'd probably win what would end up as an undignified wrestle on the ground. Besides, I was the one defending the damsel. Surely that must count for something?

I took great pride in keeping myself in good shape, but despite appearing confident, I was terrified of many things. Fighting was one of them.

Of course, things went against me, which was becoming an irritating norm in my life. The scoundrel's two friends stepped forward to support their mate. Without tapping into my limited supply of common sense, I shouted, 'I'll have you both too.'

As the words came out, they felt a little too hollow for my liking. I was digging myself in far deeper than I'd wanted to, and my voice gave me away. But I guess we can't always do the sensible thing in life. The chance to impress a pretty girl with my heroism was too much for me to resist; I couldn't back down.

Have you ever had the experience of everything slowing down and life unfolding in slow motion? Well, the next few moments were like that for me. I'd expected at least one of them to get right in my face or throw a punch at me. Instead the leader stepped back, smiled at me, and lifted up his T-shirt. What I saw tucked into his belt gave me quite a shock.

It was a pistol. And I've never seen such an expression of menacing victory in anyone's eyes. My eyes nearly came out of their sockets. The stuffing was knocked out of me, as if he'd already smacked me in the guts and suddenly I was in no-man's-land.

I felt very, very lost.

What do you do when the guy you're picking a fight with shows you a gun? What do you do when the girl who's next to you is relying on you to get her home safely?

Short of bursting into tears and begging for our lives, I had no idea. I did nothing except whisper, 'Oh.'

Then Kim whispered, 'Oh.'

Then the guy with the gun also whispered, 'Oh.'

And then he and his friends turned around and walked away.

Business as usual

The next day it was business as usual. Despite my lucky escape the evening before, nothing had changed—except now I had a good story to tell my friends at the language school. Instead of taking the hint from yet another potentially lethal drama, I spent the morning boasting about my bravery. The gods must have been looking down on me, shaking their heads. Was I ever going to take the hint? Would they have to kill me and send me back to earth again and again before I decided to wake up?

The very next evening, I decided to go out and get drunk. Drinking wasn't good for me; it never has been. I was one of those guys who got drunk, started to believe I was God's gift to women, tried to convince them of that fact, failed, and then stormed home in a huff, feeling sorry for myself. Goodness knows why

I even bothered, but idiots will be idiots, and my inflated ego still ruled my life.

A few beers and a couple of failed chat-up attempts later, I was walking home feeling sorry for myself. I was so engulfed by self-pity, I didn't notice I was hopelessly lost until I found myself heading out of town on a road I didn't recognize.

'Damn it!' I stuck my hand out to hail a taxi. At that moment three scooters shot past me with two guys on each one. They were young guys, macho guys, and I caught their attention.

Oh no, not again!

An unlit beach was on one side and deserted offices on the other. No one was around, so it wasn't a good place to meet trouble. The scooter guys pulled up and started talking to me in broken English.

'*Donde* the taxi rank is?' I asked in broken Spanish, hoping they might take pity on a lost foreigner.

'*Si*, it's on the beach. Come with us', one of them answered sarcastically.

There was no way I was going to follow these guys onto the beach. If I were lucky, they'd just take my wallet. I just kept walking up the road as they kept hovering around me on their scooters. They were keeping an eye on me, which was unnerving. Every so often they'd ride ahead of me. Just when I thought they'd lost interest, they'd turn around and cruise past me again.

After twenty minutes, I knew I was running out of time. I couldn't keep walking out of town. I needed to get to my bed. It was two in the morning, and very few cars were driving past. At the same time, my admirers were getting braver and surlier. Trouble was brewing, but I couldn't figure out how to avoid it.

If a taxi didn't come along soon, I'd have to face them—all six of them. What else could I do?

Then the gang pulled up ahead of me and turned their engines off. The silence was not golden.

Oh, God!

Time had run out. I took a deep breath and walked straight up to them. I was praying that something would stop them from mugging me—or worse. It was a surreal experience: six guys, some standing, some sitting on their scooters, staring me down. Only they and an unlit alleyway stood between me and the freedom of a taxi rank, which I could just make out in the dark. If I could look each of them in the eyes and get past them, surely they'd leave me alone?

I acted calm and walked past each of them, unconsciously holding my breath. I was past two of them, and all was well. Then I passed the third and was on to numbers four and five without any of them so much as lifting a finger. It seemed to be working. Perhaps they were just having a laugh, trying to unnerve the foreigner for a bit of sport.

But as I approached the last guy, he grabbed the arm of my leather jacket. I'd been given that jacket by an old friend of mine, and it meant a lot to me. It was soft black leather and one of the remnants of my trading days. I would have done a lot to stop it falling into the hands of some scumbag.

'Nice jacket.'

I scowled and shoved him in the chest. He let go of my jacket and did nothing else.

Phew, I thought. *I guess they're not as tough as they look.*

As I walked past the last guy, a surge of relief swept through me. I'd avoided something nasty and was still in possession of my jacket and wallet. What was it with me and guys on scooters?

I was so involved in my thoughts that I almost didn't hear two sets of footsteps running up behind me. When they caught up with me, it was too late. One of the gang grabbed me around the neck and pulled me onto my back. At the same time, another swung a punch at my head. I couldn't believe it. How could they have been so cowardly as to jump me from behind?

Arseholes!

These pricks had hassled me for half an hour and only had the guts to finish the job when I had my back turned. To make matters worse, they'd scuffed my leather jacket. That was the final straw. I stood up, and a rage far beyond anything I'd ever experienced, before or since, took over.

'Right', I yelled, pointing at the nearest one, 'I'm going to have you. I'm going to have you all.'

The power of my own voice startled me. It felt as if a giant was standing behind me screaming the words. They didn't expect such ferocity from a little guy. For a moment at least, I had the upper hand, and they started to run. It felt great to land a punch on the nearest guy. But it wasn't a good punch. It caught him on the cheek, and the cheekbone is one of the hardest parts of the body. It's not a good place to punch anyone if you want to hurt them, but I did a good job of bruising my hand. Of course I had no intention of stopping there, and I started to run towards the group.

I must have looked like a madman chasing them down the street, screaming blue murder. But it was enough to convince them to run back to their bikes and start the engines. I was so caught up in my rage that it didn't occur to me to take advantage of what had happened and get away as fast as possible. Instead I foolishly ran after them, intent on teaching them a lesson they'd never forget.

Finally!

Running towards the scooter gang surprised me almost as much as it did them. Despite appearing quite heroic, I can't take credit for my apparent bravery. It was just anger clouding my judgment, which gave me courage I didn't normally possess. However, it also gave me the upper hand for a few valuable seconds.

In those few seconds, it became clear that if I kept after them I was getting myself into deep water, and that the courage could drain from my bones as quickly as it arrived. The gang hadn't seen I was half drunk and as soft as a cream doughnut. But they would, and as soon as they did, they'd beat seven bells out of me. Cutting my losses, I turned around and ran away down the dark street as fast as I could.

An hour later I lay in my bed, staring at the ceiling and wondering if I'd woken up my miserable Spanish family by crashing into my room at three in the morning. My thoughts drifted to what had just happened, to the gun episode, the scooters, and yet another close shave. I'd been so lucky to escape in one piece. Then my thoughts drifted to Cornwall and I recalled my not-so-near-death 'shark' encounter, smiling as I remembered what a wimp I'd been. And finally, I felt the terror of being trapped on a Welsh mountainside with Mark.

As I relived all these events in my mind, I wondered if there was any significance in them. Was it just wild coincidence that I'd experienced so much drama in a few short months? My life had always had its ups and downs, but this was beginning to get out of hand. I wracked my brain to find an answer, yet none came.

I had no clue. My hand hurt, I was probably going to be thrown out of my lodgings, and a big hangover was waiting for me. I decided to stop fighting with my thoughts and give in.

It was then, lying on an uncomfortable bed in Spain, staring into a blackness beyond my mind, that I let go of all my thoughts and a deep peace emerged from within me. Oh my

God! Peace wasn't something I experienced in those days, yet there was something very familiar about this state. It was simple, yet so quiet that it seemed to stretch on forever, and I felt so at home with it. Although I was a thousand miles from Scotland, living with the Spanish equivalent of the Addams family, I felt at home. I felt as if I were resting in the depth of my being. All my thoughts and worries left me, dwarfed by this deep presence of peace. It is so hard to put it into words, yet so lovely to experience. I became like space, like air, free, without restriction or worries.

In this letting go, clarity came to me. These dramas weren't isolated coincidences; they'd been trying to tell me something. Life had been trying to give me a message. When I hadn't listened, it had smacked me over the head, again and again. It was trying to tell me I was going in the wrong direction.

Amidst that deep, embracing peace, it dawned on me that somehow I was creating all this drama. Although that responsibility seemed scary, it also meant I had the power to change things. I hadn't managed to find lasting happiness by changing the circumstances of my life, but perhaps I could find it by going within myself.

In that moment it became clear just how ignorant I'd been. I'd known that, more than anything, I wanted to be happy, but I hadn't done what was required to find happiness. The chaos in my life had accelerated after my encounter with the shiatsu guy who'd told me about that meditation practice. He'd told me only days after I prayed for help, but I ignored his words. Perhaps this ancient meditation was the solution to my problems?

I wasn't sure if I was right or wrong, but there was only one way to find out. I needed to return to England and learn this practice and see for myself. I just had to do it. So the next day, I packed in my disastrous Spanish course and flew home.

By a stroke of luck, there was an Ishayas of the Bright Path Ascension course a few days later in Glastonbury. I booked myself a place. I hoped the techniques would be a bit easier to master than the name! When I got off the phone with the course organizer, I chuckled to myself. I'd been so stubborn. Ever since the shiatsu guy had told me about this Ascension I had known that I was meant to learn, but it had taken four smacks for me to realize. At last I was going to find out what this was all about. I could have been hard on myself about how stubborn I had been, but instead I just laughed, it was easier. What I didn't know at the time was that although my stubbornness had caused me many problems, it would become invaluable for my journey within.

I didn't know much about Glastonbury, other than that there's a huge performing arts festival there every year; the place is almost as famous for the mud as the music. I didn't know anything about these Ascension techniques. The shiatsu guy had told me about them, but I'd blocked that information from my memory. Intense boredom tended to make me do that.

But what did I have to lose? If it didn't work, then at least I'd have a nice trip to the countryside. And if it did work, well I wasn't really sure what would happen, other than that life was going to get better. At least that's what I hoped!

The course

As I sat on the train staring out of the window, I felt glad that I'd made a decision. But I also started to wonder what I was getting myself into. Meditation was a hippy thing, wasn't it?

Would the people on the course be a bunch of dreadlocked, hemp-cardigan-wearing, dope-smoking dropouts moaning about pollution and the state of the environment? I certainly hoped not. I had lived with a group of hippies in Australia and managed to mortally offend them by cooking up steaks and sausages when all they ate was lentils and green beans.

Then another thought struck me. *How the hell am I going to meditate for a whole weekend?* I found it hard enough to sit through an episode of *EastEnders*.

I was unaware of it at the time, but I was about to embark on the greatest adventure of my life. It was an adventure that would be far more rewarding than I could have imagined. I was about to start on what the ancients call the 'path of heroes.' The final frontier of investigating my own mind, and then moving beyond it. Little me was about to set out on the greatest adventure which exists, the journey within.

The course organizer, Felicia, an intense forty-something woman with curly black hair, picked me up at the station. She seemed pleasant enough until she got onto the road, where she revealed an intimate relationship with road rage. Blasting her horn and cursing the other drivers as we belted along the quiet country lanes, she seemed more interested in lecturing them on their driving habits than paying much attention to the road.

As we hurtled along at Mach 3, I stupidly asked her a lot of questions, as much to keep my attention off her driving as to make polite conversation.

The first thing she explained was that she'd used Ascension to overcome her anger issues. I hoped she was joking.

Then she said, 'The weekend course is called the First Sphere. You learn four techniques based on praise, gratitude, love,

72

and compassion, and they'll help you to be happy.' Her voice was surprisingly soft, especially considering that her car was almost on two wheels as it skidded around a bend.

'Are *you* happy?' I asked her through gritted teeth.

'Mmm. Well, I'm a lot happier than I was before I learned. I wouldn't say I'm completely at peace, as you can see by my driving'—she gave me a wink—'but my life is getting better, and I'm learning to laugh at myself. I'm more relaxed and creative, and yes, I do feel happier. I feel a lot more myself these days.'

'But how do you quiet your mind? I have so many thoughts, I could never stop them.' I asked, hoping that I would survive long enough to actually learn to Ascend.

'Me too', she said, grinning. 'With this you don't need to resist anything you experience—that's the key. Thoughts and emotions are okay. It's so much easier to find peace if you are not fighting with your mind, and just let it do what it does.' What she said seemed to make sense to me, yet I was not convinced.

'Who's teaching the course?'

'The Ishayas. They're monks who have dedicated their lives to raising consciousness.'

'What does that mean?'

'I asked the same question when I learned', she said. 'It means making the world a better place. If one person becomes happier, it affects the people around him or her. It creates more happiness. The Ishayas do this through meditation.'

'How many people are going to the course?' I asked, hoping that there would be a fun bunch of people on the weekend.

'This is a small course. There's just you and a girl on it, but some people who have already learned will be popping in to repeat it. Once you've learned, you can repeat it for free. The Ishayas are more interested in helping people find peace than making millions', she told me, squinting her eyes as she tried to figure out if she could overtake a mini Cooper on the blind corner that we were approaching. After three years in the city, this sounded like a refreshing approach, but my mind kept churning. *Monks? What would they be like? Would they have long brown cassocks and bald heads with bowl-cut fringes? Perhaps a Bible or two knocking around?*

I smiled as images of Canon Hammock came back to me. *I hope they're a bit more relaxed than he was.*

'So, this is some kind of religious thing?' I asked.

'No, it's not a belief system—it's all about experiencing more peace. You don't have to believe in anything to learn it. They don't teach you new beliefs. They just give you the tools to find your own happiness. It's very old, and there's more to it than meets the eye.'

Her bumper passed within inches of a tractor. 'Idiot!' she screamed. 'Sorry.' She smiled sheepishly.

I didn't understand how monks couldn't be religious, but I decided to let it go.

By some miracle we got to her home in one piece. As I carried my rucksack through the front door, I met the first of the two Ishaya monks. He took up almost the whole doorway, like some grizzly bear blocking the sun. 'Samadeva. Pleased to meet ya.'

He beamed as he offered me a paw. I took to him instantly. It was impossible not to like someone with a smile that big. Then the other Ishaya, a small cat-like woman, introduced herself as Rodavi. She was shy, but there was something pleasant and peaceful about her.

I was to learn over the weekend that these monks were not your everyday, run-of-the-mill monks. They'd dedicated their lives to finding peace within themselves and helping others do the same. But they lived in the real world and had real jobs. They were both quite different, yet there was something similar about them. They had a joy, an inner confidence, a certain something which I liked and hadn't seen often in my life.

Despite their funny names, they were surprisingly normal. Samadeva, judging by the size of him and his enthusiasm at meal times, liked the good life. He was an American, an ex-GI. Rodavi was skinny, drank black coffee as if it were going out of fashion, and had a bizarre fascination with old cemetaries. Insisting that she wasn't religious, she assured me that graveyards were very peaceful places, and that as long as she was in England she'd get to as many as she could. She seemed to be the most radical of the pair, dressing in black all the time and not eating much. But her friendly smile allayed my initial fears that she might be a devil worshipper.

Both Samadeva and Rodavi had a terrific sense of humour. They seemed to be walking their talk and living a joyful life. Whenever I sat in the kitchen of the small terraced house in Glastonbury chatting away to Samadeva, I couldn't help but enjoy the big guy's company enormously. I enjoyed it even when we weren't talking. He was so relaxed that I felt something different when he was around. I couldn't quite put my finger on it, but he had something I wanted. This X factor would become very familiar to me as I met more and more Ishayas over the years.

'That's the presence you feel', he said to me, apparently reading my mind. He went on. 'Once you've been Ascending for a while, you become way more peaceful and other people can feel it.'

'How did you know what I was thinking?'

'I didn't, really, but as you keep Ascending your intuition gets keener and keener. You just kinda know things.'

Before I could ask him more about this, a young woman walked into the room. She was also taking the course, and her name was Mars.

Oh my God! I thought. *Not another weird name.*

She was dressed in a green sweater with a rainbow-coloured beanie over her dreadlocked head. Mars was a singer from Australia, and despite my reservations about hippies, I liked her. That she had beautiful eyes and sang like an angel certainly helped too.

The first evening of the First Sphere course was pretty straightforward. I could have listened to the Ishayas talk all day, even if they'd been discussing paint. They were telling me what I already knew, but in the busyness of life I'd forgotten. It's incredible how enjoyable it is to hear people who are happy talk about happiness.

However, when it came to actually meditating, or Ascending as they called it, the weekend took a turn for the worse.

My first experience of Ascending wasn't anything to write home about. I sat on a comfy sofa in the homely sitting room in Glastonbury, quite looking forward to trying out this Ascension thing. But as soon as I closed my eyes, my head exploded with thoughts. I have no idea what I thought about, but my mind didn't stop. The fifteen minutes felt like two hours, and I reckon I must have thought about almost everything it was humanly possible to think of. When Samadeva finally told us to open our eyes, I breathed a sigh of relief.

'How was it? How was your first Ascension?' he asked innocently. I paused for a moment.

'Well, kind of boring. I felt frustrated and bored. I had thousands of thoughts all the time. It felt like we were Ascending for hours', I said, feeling a bit guilty for moaning.

All I'd wanted to do for the whole Ascension was run away and play a video game, anything to take my mind off the bloody meditation. I was regretting coming on this course. When there were so many fun things to do, why would I want to close my eyes and experience that?

To make matters worse, Mars started to talk. 'That was amazing! I saw a bright, golden light appear over my crown chakra. Then someone—it sounded like an angel—started to sing to me. It was the most beautiful song I've ever heard. It was magical. It's given me a great idea for a new song.'

Tears streamed down her cheeks as she shared this profound experience, and I shrank into the sofa, pretending not to be there. I was disgusted. How come the unemployed hippy could do it so well and I just had loads of thoughts?

Bugger it, I thought. I'd really hoped that this course was going to save me. It was my last resort, but it didn't work. How could I have been so stupid as to think a weekend course could make a difference to my whole life?

'It's normal to have thoughts and emotions when you Ascend, particularly if you've been a bit stressed out. Don't worry about it—it'll get easier. It won't be like that every time', Samadeva reassured me.

The big guy seemed to understand. Then he uttered those words which had been haunting me for the past few months: 'Just hang in there. If you do this, you'll find more peace and joy, and your life will become easier. You just gotta do it. No matter how it feels, it works anyway.'

That encouraged me a bit, but I was far from convinced. But what choice did I have? I was on the course, stuck in the middle of the Cotswolds, so I figured I might as well jump in with both feet. After all, it was only my first go, and it would probably get easier. I wasn't going to let a bit of boredom stop me from finding happiness.

Some people want a quick fix to their problems, something which doesn't involve much commitment. They want everything but aren't prepared to give very much. I wasn't one of those people; I liked a challenge. I liked the idea of setting off on a journey to clean my nervous system of stress and heal my relationship with my mind. The promise of eventually finding endless peace sounded great too.

Back at the First Sphere course, Mars continued to tell us about her mind-blowing experiences, which got more and more impressive each time. My experience stayed the same, boring and thought filled. I was disgusted.

Finally, as I wandered onto Glastonbury

Tor on the Sunday afternoon of the course, I finally experienced my own bit of magic. I noticed that the world looked a bit different. A wizened old tree I usually wouldn't have given a second glance caught my eye. As I looked around, I could have sworn that the countryside had become more beautiful, more alive. *Wow!*

Of course, the countryside was just the same as it had been before, but I was different. I was seeing more beauty. At the same time, I also noticed that my mind was quiet. I was peaceful, unconcerned by the normal thoughts and worries which went through my head. It was hard to believe. It was so simple to be at peace, yet I'd spent most of my life being anything but. I was actually starting to enjoy just being, without having to entertain myself with thinking about stuff. Was this the end of boredom for me?

I was getting a taste of the present moment, and I liked it. And it wasn't just some idea I read about in a book; I was living it. Now, after just two days of Ascending, I was starting to see the world differently and finding some freedom. Praise the Lord! There was a God!

That experience spurred me on. It may have been boring to Ascend with my eyes closed, but the Ishayas told me that the feeling was just the result of stress leaving my nervous system. Having a bit of boredom in return for de-stressing my whole body didn't seem like a big price to pay. And when I did it with my eyes, open I felt great. So I did it every day.

The Path of Joy

As you know, when I learned to Ascend I wasn't a particularly happy guy. I wasn't totally miserable either, but I didn't cope very well with the external pressures of life or the internal pressures of my own mental programming. I experienced quite a lot of fear, which I covered up by being over confident. Yet at other times in my life I was a pretty happy go lucky kind of guy. I guess like many of us I had my ups and downs. But I rarely gave myself time to stop and reflect. I remember being a happy child, but as I grew older I had learned to think—just like you and probably everyone you know. I became lost in the thoughts of my mind and left my naturally happy state.

I grew up into an adult who was often angry and afraid, a man who judged the world and the people in it. I had a habit of keeping myself very busy, never really relaxing. This was probably because I was scared of what I might feel if I ever stopped to look. My default mode was to find something to occupy myself with, and I became a high achiever. I poured so much energy into whatever I did that success usually followed. I used to pride myself in being able to push myself to success. I pushed myself to get good grades at school. I pushed myself to become a broker. I pushed myself to run marathons. If I didn't push myself, how would I achieve success? And if I wasn't successful, who would respect me? Who would love me? As soon as I achieved one goal, another appeared, and then another and another. I was like a rat on a wheel. As long as I kept running, I got fed and watered, and I survived.

But with my successes came little internal stability. I was tossed around by my emotions, my thoughts, my fears, and my worries. My relationships were full of drama. I needed confirmation that I was okay, and that must have been exhausting for my partners. Exhausting and not very sexy!

I always tried to put aside time for the important things, the parts of life which mattered to me. Yet when I did, I was rarely present. My body was there, sitting in the fancy restaurant with my family and friends. But I was always somewhere else in my head, thinking, *How am I going to deal with Dave's strategy meeting tomorrow?*

I would be thinking constantly as I chewed on the finest steak without even tasting it. The thoughts in my head demanded my attention most of the time. They took me away from being present in my life. I spent the best years of my life entangled in my mind, oblivious to the present moment and how good it felt to be alive.

In reality, I was living life in a cage. I was a prisoner, in the most maximum of maximum-security prisons. The reason it was so difficult to escape from was that I didn't even know it existed.

Don't get me wrong. I had a pretty good life. I had a lot of adventures and fun too, but I often had a nagging sense that something was wrong—with me, with the world, and with the way things were. I'd had the feeling since I was very young that I was meant to do something good with my life. I've met many people who knew they were here on earth to do something good. Something significant. Something different. Perhaps you're one of them. But I didn't know what to do, and being a success in the business world hadn't cut it. As it was, I was really just surviving. But surviving is very different from living. Most of us are quite good at surviving, but how many of us really live?

Back then I believed that how well things in my world were going caused me happiness or pain. I relied on my life going the way I wanted it to or I was unhappy. Of course I was trying to create a life which made me happy.

When I went to the course in Glastonbury, I remember thinking that it all sounded a bit too good to be true. I wanted to believe the Ishayas when they told me that peace and joy were my birthright, but it sounded pretty unlikely that a bit of meditating was going to make such a big difference to me. Yet, despite my doubts it was happening anyway!

Fortunately, those chaotic Ascensions I experienced at first didn't last forever. They never do. It took a bit of time, but my experience of Ascending and, more importantly, my experience of life, changed quite dramatically.

After a few weeks of practice, I started to notice the peaceful place inside me more often, sometimes when I had my eyes closed during Ascending and sometimes in my daily life. When I first discovered this new way of being, it was so subtle that often I didn't even notice it. It was like a feeling of an empty space inside me, so light it could easily be overlooked. But whenever it was there, I was happy and not worried about anything. Over time I became more familiar with it. I started to notice that whenever I was stressed, I'd forgotten about this space and I could use the Ascension techniques to find it again. In short, I was learning to make a different choice, a choice which started to make my life so much easier and 'in the flow.'

Sometimes I even woke up happy for no reason at all. I started to sleep more deeply and wake up feeling rested, which was such a relief. It felt as if my brain was being calmed down, but at the same time, I also felt more alive. My soul was getting a warm bath!

The more I learned to be in this state, the less power my fears and worries seemed to have over me. Unsurprisingly, as my judgments have fallen away, the world I see now has changed for the better too. People seem to be nicer, and many of my relationships are richer.

I've discovered that people who are fearful see a scary world. Happy people tend to see a friendlier world. It's the same world, but people experience it very differently. I'd been wearing dark glasses which made the world appear much worse than it was. Now

I've taken those glasses off.

I didn't really appreciate it at the time, but I'd stumbled upon a path to true happiness. It wasn't some self-development course that helped me make more money or improved my relationship with pot plants, but something which allowed me to access a different state of consciousness. Which is a whole different ball game. It's a state which is unaffected by worries, stress, or anxiety, a state where I feel free. The practice had given me the key to unlocking what I believe everyone really wants: happiness and joy. It's not the kind of happiness I used to feel when the Scotland rugby team won a match (which alas was not very often in those days), but a state which is there no matter how my life's going.

I discovered and continue to discover many profound things. It became clear to me that to truly live, you need to be at peace. I learned that finding peace isn't about getting rid of emotions or thoughts. What we put our attention on grows. If we allow our attention to be on the peaceful presence within, that grows too. There's no need to struggle to quiet the mind or reject feelings and emotions. Once you've found an inner peace, then you can accept, enjoy, or change the circumstances of life. But until you find that peace, I have found that life lacks a certain meaning and vitality.

As well, happiness isn't found in the life we lead or the successes we enjoy. It's found internally, as a state of inner quiet and presence. Strangely enough, it can exist even when life doesn't go our way. True happiness is found within us. It's available whether we're on the beach or in a board meeting. Said in another way, finding happiness isn't about rearranging our lives; it's about changing our relationship with our thoughts and emotions.

The Ishayas taught me that I didn't need to change my life to be happy. I didn't need to have a special diet or meditate cross-legged in the mountains. I didn't need to force myself to think positively. It didn't matter if I was a Christian, a Muslim, an atheist, or even Welsh: I could still find peace.

They told me that Ascension wasn't a belief system or a strict set of rules. It was a practical way to find happiness. I stopped pushing myself and started to learn that it's far more effective to go with the flow of life than to force it.

I discovered that inner peace brings with it a flexibility and pragmatism. Most importantly, it also brings an ability to laugh at yourself. The journey of discovering who we are is much easier if we can laugh at ourselves. It's no longer little me against the world.

But it hasn't all been skipping joyfully

along the path of life. I was also to discover that it takes commitment to find peace. It was quite easy for me to make excuses to do other things with my time, to avoid my twenty minutes of Ascending to wash the dishes or call a friend. But I also didn't find it too hard to fit it into my days. I usually felt so much better afterwards that it seemed crazy not to make the time. I was becoming so much more relaxed and easy-going, much to the relief of my family and friends!

At times I did get a bit disheartened, especially if I had a few thought-filled or emotional Ascensions, or was going through tough times in my personal life, because then I used to doubt if it was still working for me. It would have been so easy for me to give up, but although I was many things, I wasn't a quitter who wimped out when the going got tough. I knew what I wanted. I wanted to be free from suffering and to experience more and more love in my life. I was pretty sure Ascension would bring that experience to me if I persisted, so I kept going. I did what's perhaps most important on any path to peace: I didn't give up. Continuing with this practice turned out to be the best decision of my life.

We all have different paths to walk. Sometimes they can be swift and easy, and sometimes there can be challenges. Sometimes life can be bloody difficult. But if you can find a way to reconnect with your natural state of inner happiness and you have the guts to keep going, it seems to work out. No matter what life throws at you, it is possible to get through it and come out the other side.

Now, things are rather different for me. I've gone from being a stressed-out broker to being a peaceful Ishaya monk. I replaced my frenetic London lifestyle with a more relaxed life in Oslo. Yet the change in my circumstances is nothing compared to the change in how I experience life itself.

The Presence within

For much of my life, I'd been wearing an invisible suit of armour. I'd presented an 'I've got it together' image, yet the truth was far from that. I was quite good at acting as if I'd got it together, but inside I was often confused, scared, or frustrated. Now I was taking off the armour, piece by piece.

As this armour fell away, something new yet somehow familiar entered my life. My racing mind, which used to drive me so crazy, calmed down. At the same time, I started to notice a presence within me which I could describe as a kind of nothingness or space. This presence was still and unmoving. I couldn't see it, but I could experience it. Whenever it was there, I was reminded of those times in my life when I'd felt most happy and safe. I'd experienced it a lot as a child, but as I grew up, I forgot about it.

Strangely, this simple presence revealed itself as the key to experiencing what I really wanted, lasting happiness.

I believe that this presence is in itself the elusive Holy Grail. It's not an ancient cup hidden in the depths of Mesopotamia but an experience of heaven on earth, or the profound happiness which Jesus talked about. It was no different from the state of nirvana which Buddha spoke of.

It seemed that the more I tapped into it, the better my life became—not always in an obvious way, like being showered with gifts or getting exactly what I wanted, but in deeper, more subtle ways. I became more sensitive to situations, more in tune with myself. It became easier to be happy and joyful. I was remembering who I really was. I was no longer some guy struggling to make it in the world, but a content, alive person who wasn't shaken by the ups and downs of life. The magic of being alive started to become more obvious. Praise, gratitude, love, and compassion grew within me.

Being with the presence is a surprisingly simple and familiar state which many of us drop into it from time to time, often when we're driving or doing something we enjoy where we don't have to think much. Athletes call it 'the zone.' Getting acquainted with it, diving into it, and uniting with it is a real adventure. Does being able to reach this state make me superhuman? Can I fly? Can I read people's minds and blow fire out of my bottom?

Nope.

I'm a pretty ordinary guy who lives a pretty ordinary life. Yet I'm happier than I ever thought I'd be. I find so much enjoyment in the simple things, the things which matter. The presence continues to grow, and with it the ease and enjoyment of my life. I'm told that I can explore this state and live from it for the rest of my days.

Somehow, little old me stumbled upon what I believe most people are looking for: the path to the Holy Grail. Yet it happened more by chance than by skill or cunning. Perhaps I'd accrued good karma in some other lifetime. Or perhaps I was just so desperately lost and my desire for peace was so strong that I was prepared to do anything to get it. Whatever the reasons, I discovered what *you* probably want more than anything. This short book is my way of sharing that with you.

It's a bold statement to claim that I know what you want. It's not meant to sound conceited. I could be wrong. You might want a Ferrari more than anything. You might want success or good health. You might want happiness for your family or even the whole world. But chances are if you get any of these things, they'd only make you feel happy for a short time, so perhaps what you really want more than anything is true happiness, and not just for yourself but for the impact is has on others.

A few months after I learned to Ascend, I travelled to Australia. A friend of mine who lived there was a girl called Jess. Jess had noticed a lot of improvements in her life, and was very committed to Ascending. She told me she wanted to become an Ishaya monk, and to teach Ascension to other people. I had no idea what being an Ishaya involved, other than getting a strange new name. From what she told me, the Ishayas were normal people who'd dedicated their lives to finding more peace and happiness within themselves. Then they helped that happiness spread into the world and the people around them. Their job was to live their lives from deeper levels of peace and to serve humanity in any way which brought them joy. The name *Ishaya* is a Sanskrit word and means 'for the highest consciousness' or 'the highest love.'

'If one person becomes happier, it affects the people around them', she told me with a big grin.

If that's true—and science seems to be

confirming it is—then each of us has a far greater impact on the world than we may realize. By finding peace, we make the world a much better place. We contribute in perhaps the most positive way possible. And our reward? More peace, joy and happiness!

'People are more like popcorn than you might think. Once one of us pops, it's easier for the rest to do the same', she once said. My blank expression must have said it all.

'Okay, how can I explain it? If you hang out with angry people, you're more likely to be angry or afraid, yes? If you hang out with happy people, you laugh and enjoy yourself more. You get the picture. If enough of us find peace, then we can change the world. We can literally help the world find peace just by finding it in ourselves.' I loved it when she talked like that, I hadn´t heard many people explain life in such a clear and pure way. Her words made some sense to me, but I was still skeptical.

'Even if you don´t agree with me', she said, 'physics does. It's proven we're all connected, and that the magnetic fields or energy we emit affects everything around us. If you look at the problems of the world and try to figure them out, it fries your brain. But if you see you can affect the underlying level of love and harmony and raise it, then you have *real* power to make a difference. It's so exciting! Raising the level of love or consciousness in the world helps everything. It's the difference between curing a problem and just putting a plaster on it and hoping for the best. You're either part of the solution or part of the problem, depending on whether you're happy or suffering. That's why I want to become an Ishaya. I want to make a real difference.'

In those days I wasn't interested in becoming an Ishaya. There seemed to be far too many other interesting things to do with my life than become a monk. But I was intruiged.

'Monks invented coffee and beer', she once told me with an air of victory, and I became more open to the idea.

Strangely enough Jess never became an Ishaya. But after a few months of bumming around Australia, I felt the pull to become one myself. I went away to a retreat in the hills just outside Kelowna in Canada, where I Ascended for six months, played a bit of volleyball and table tennis, and met some lovely people. I went to lots of interesting meetings and some very boring ones too, but I felt welcomed and accepted by the Ishayas. It was so good to be around other people who were committed to happiness.

When I left Canada I was in a much better state than when I'd arrived. Unlike some of the high achievers, I wouldn't say I'd found permanent inner peace, but I was on the way. I enjoyed being part of a group of people interested in raising the level of consciousness of the planet and creating more love and peace in the world, especially as they were such a strange and diverse group from so many different walks of life. There were housewives, house husbands, lawyers, accountants, motorcycle shop owners, children, doctors, surgeons, writers, poets, the unemployed, actors, opera singers, and teachers. In their own ways, they were dedicated to helping people find peace in their busy lives. Some did it by teaching Ascension and others by just living a happy life and showing others it was possible.

It hasn't always been the easiest thing to be dedicated to. Life can throw up challenges, and being willing to find peace in tricky situations requires courage and dedication. I haven't always had an easy journey, and at times it's felt bloody difficult. But by remembering what I want more than anything and being willing to go for it, help has always arrived when I needed it most, and the joy and ease of life has returned.

Some people avoid finding inner

happiness because they're convinced that focusing so much on your own happiness makes you a selfish person. However, I see it differently. If you're genuinely pursuing peace, you become more giving, loving, patient, and kind. Usually the desire to serve the common good becomes stronger. People who are unhappy or live in fear don't usually contribute much which is positive to society. They can't; they're too busy just trying to survive. But someone who's at peace can move mountains and catalyse huge positive changes. I believe that to be a really good parent, partner, or friend, it really helps to be happy.

My own life these days is happy but far from sedate. I have a teenage stepson, and a fiancée who works full-time and needs to be fed, watered, and massaged. I also teach Ascension, give talks, write, and meet with people who are on their spiritual path. Yet even when I'm very busy, there's usually a flow and ease most of the time, a sense of gratitude for being alive.

Is it necessary to become an Ishaya monk to find peace? No. Since I was very young, I wanted to have a positive impact on the world, so it felt quite natural for me to become one. But it's certainly not required. However, what is required to find lasting happiness is discovering it within you.

The voices in our heads

I guess you've heard the jokes about people who listen to voices in their heads. They're the people we tend to think of as mad. But here's a funny thing. We all have those voices in our heads, and most of us listen to them all day.

What am I going to have for supper?
Oh, I gotta phone Sue.
Damn, I forgot to phone Sue.
I don't think Sue likes me anymore.

Chat, chat, chat, chat. They chatter away for much of the day. Sometimes the voices are commenting on the weather, our bad backs, problems at work, or the state of the country or world. Other times they're telling us what we need to do next, or who likes us and who doesn't. They tell us who to trust and who not to trust. They tell us whether we look good today, or whether we need to lose more weight. They advise us what to do and what not to do. The voices don't care what they talk about, as long as they have our attention. They're a bit like spoilt children; they live and thrive off our attention.

It may or may not be news to you, but not only do we all have many different voices in our heads, but we also listen to them, chat to them, and even argue with them! It's the same the whole world over. Most of us are in fact quite loopy to some degree or other. We just don't know it (or we don't admit it). If we did at least know it, then we might be able to do something about it. But most of us are so used to those voices that we think they're part of us. It's quite bizarre, really.

If you don't believe me that voices constantly fill your head, just cast your mind back to the last time you had an argument with someone. Then think about how long the argument continued, even after you and the other person parted company. Sometimes our arguments can go on for weeks in our minds as we try to think up better things to say, or the voices replay the same scenario again and again. How annoying it is to find the perfect comeback ten minutes too late!

And just think of those times when someone has cut you up on the road, and for the rest of the day you ponder it and even get angry about it. Although the incident was over in seconds, the aftermath lasts for a lot longer.

Our voices comment on our lives and our worlds most of the time. But these voices have no innate authority. There's no good reason to listen to them. They aren't wise, although they may pretend to be. They don't necessarily have our best interests at heart; they're just thought patterns based on our experiences of life. They can be wolves in sheep's clothing, as they often give us information which is out of date or just wrong. Even though they're just thoughts and nothing more, we listen to them, value them, *and* give them power over us. How else can we live?

The answer is by intuition. By refining and developing our natural knowing, the answers in life come more easily and accurately. Living from refined intuition is far more effective than mulling things over in your mind, bouncing from possible solution, to problem, to analysis.

Have you ever had a problem you were trying to figure out for days? It just occupied your mind for so long, it became confusing and boring. Finally you thought, *To hell with it!* and decided to stop thinking about it. *Bang!* The answer came from nowhere. That was your own experience of using intuition rather than linear thinking, and it worked! Our thoughts may convince us that we need them, but their help is highly overrated. Fortunately, it's quite easy to discover that thoughts are very 'last year'!

Thousands of thoughts pass through our heads every day, and most of them have nothing to do with what's in front of us. Some take us into the past, so we regret things we've done or haven't done. Or they take us into the future, so we plan and worry. Have you ever lain in bed worrying about how work would go the next day? Think of the times you may have worried about stuff, sometimes for weeks. Perhaps it was a job interview, a health problem, or a bill. Then after all that stress, everything turned out okay. The bad thing never happened! You wasted so much energy and time on a hypothetical situation which never came to pass. Mark Twain summed it up perfectly when he said, 'I have had thousands of problems in my life, and most of them have never happened.'

Worrying about the future is an example of listening to those voices, and it leads to a certain degree of suffering and unease, as does not attending to the present. Have you ever found it hard to follow a conversation because your mind was wondering about other things? Many of us don't participate in large chunks of our lives because of this. We may be very sociable, hard workers, and good parents, but we don't usually give our full attention to what's going on right now. Our bodies are there, but our minds are all over the place. Think of a time when you were taking a holiday or spending time with your most uplifting friends, yet you were miserable. Despite being in a situation which should have been great, it was more like chewing plastic—a bit dull. We leave ourselves open to suffering because of the voices and the emotions in our head. The best parts of our lives can just pass us by.

Of course, some of the voices seem nice. Some of them tell us things like the following:

Ah, I'm doing great.

I look wonderful.

But just as easily, the same voice can become mean. They can be transformed in the blink of an eye and become cruel:

There's no way I can do that.

I'm not good enough.

I'll never get over that.

Life is hard—that's just the way it is.

Think of some of the creative ideas you've had but never done anything with because your mind told you, 'No way, I can't do that. It won't work.' If we believe these negative voices, then we're living our life in a cage. We're prisoners. It's not that we don't necessarily have a good life; it's just that we're not fully living it. We're not free.

So apart from listening to our intuition, is there anything more we can do instead of listening to the voices? Luckily there is. The alternative is to find the still presence which exists within you and build up a relationship with that. This 'still place' is very close, closer than your next breath. It is peaceful and alive. Yet many of us have forgotten about it, or have at least forgotten how to find it. The good news is that it hasn't gone anywhere. It's waiting inside all of us, patiently waiting to be rediscovered.

Do you really want peace?

I've been lucky enough to ask many people what they want more than anything. It's fascinating to hear their replies. Most people answer that they want peace or happiness, with love as the number three answer. But often those who claim they want peace, happiness, or love don't want it enough to do anything about it.

Yes, saying you want peace sounds like a tasty idea, kind of sweet like chocolate. And saying it's something you want is easy to do at a seminar or in a discussion. Yet in order to find it, you have to want it and then be willing to do something about it. Some people want to read or hear about the 'chocolate', but they're not that interested in tasting it for themselves.

We put lots of time and effort into our jobs, our families, and our health, but not usually our peace. But no matter how well my job, family, or health was going, no matter how many exciting things I was doing in my life, none of these things ever gave me permanent peace. They gave me moments, perhaps days, of relative happiness. They gave me a feeling of connection and being part of something. But these moments faded all too quickly, and the worries crept in once again. Permanent happiness rarely, if ever, is found in the happenings of the world. It's found within.

Even if my cunning plan had worked out and I'd moved to Thailand, it was never going to make me happy. Living on the beach would have been nice for a while. But wherever I go, I take my thoughts with me, so I still would have been listening to those negative thoughts in my head.

Have you ever been on holiday, got yourself comfy on a lounger by the pool, and enjoyed the feeling of freedom and relaxation? There's no need to think about your problems, but within twenty minutes your mind has already started finding them: the waiter's too slow, the sun's too hot, and some kids next to you are making too much noise. Your mind has spoiled your holiday even before it's really started.

I don't believe there's anything wrong

with having money or success. This book isn't a call for you to quit your job; it's an invitation to really live your life, free from suffering. I've often wondered if I would have enjoyed being a trader if I'd found peace beforehand. Perhaps, perhaps not. I just don't know. But from what I've seen, anyone who believes that either money or success alone brings you lasting happiness is kidding themselves. I had pretty much everything I wanted. I had money, good friends, and a supportive family, and I lived in a lovely flat in Wimbledon. I had so much, but I was unable to enjoy it because I listened to the thoughts in my head—the moaning and whingeing—most of the day.

Through Ascension, I got to see what makes me tick. I discovered that the thoughts influenced and controlled me. I learnt to see the thoughts in my head as just thoughts, not facts. It gave me the freedom to act from my own intuition, which I've found is far more reliable than I ever knew. As I listened to them less and less, more and more happiness arrived.

Has it all been roses and skipping through life with a smile on my face since I learned to Ascend? No! But I think it's very normal to feel stressed, disillusioned, or discouraged at times when you're on a path of self-discovery. But I was lucky, or at least I took my chances when I recognized them. I was given the support and the tools to move through my challenges. When we look within ourselves, we discover many incredible things. We also meet our fears. This can be tough, but with the correct guidance and support, it need never be too much for us.

If you really want peace, you don't need to look any further. Ascension is a way to experience it. It's just a question of whether you *really* want it, or whether you want to wait and postpone your happiness.

It takes motivation to do it, dedication really. Yet if you recognize that to be really happy and free is what you want, it *is* attainable. 'The Kingdom of Heaven is at hand. Seek it first and all else will be given unto you.'

By desiring to be truly happy, being willing to change, and then going for it wholeheartedly, anyone can find a peace which is solid.

Conclusion

As I've mentioned, I believe I've found what most people are looking for. I was lucky enough to see that it's far more important to be happy than it is to be successful. That's not to say that the two can't be combined. The world needs sensitive and aware doctors, happy business people, and peaceful pilots. But if you had to choose between the two, happiness would be a good bet.

All the success and riches in the world mean very little if you wake up miserable every morning. Whether you're the most successful businesswoman, the greatest football player, or a homeless guy on the street, if you're not at peace then the gift of life is being wasted. It's equally true that if you're pious and spiritual, and you eat all the right foods and read all the right books but you're not at peace, you're also missing out on life too.

I believe *you* probably want peace, joy, fulfillment, happiness, and contentment more than anything. And you might claim you want material things, fame, or success more than that. But if you got those things, how would you feel? Happy? Alive? Content?

Perhaps you would for a while, but quite quickly life would return to how it was before. I reckon what you really want is happiness, and perhaps the condo in Hawaii is just a way of getting a taste of that.

I have discovered that no one can make anyone else happy, not even the most exciting partner or project, the best job, the greatest holiday, or even the most prolific achievements. You could invent the cure for all disease or solve the world's food shortage, but it wouldn't give you permanent happiness. The way to find that is to look for it as a state within you. Thank goodness, because it's a lot easier than achieving all these other things!

This book can't show you how to find peace; no book can do that. It usually requires a method and the guidance of others who have already walked the path. The most effective way I know of is to find some sort of meditation which takes you to the silent presence within.

If it all sounds a bit daunting, ask yourself, 'Am I someone who really wants peace? Or do I just talk a good game?'

Or put another way, 'Do I want to taste the chocolate or just think about it?'

Peace is inside everyone, just waiting to be discovered. There's no one too stupid or too clever, too rich or too poor, or too good or too bad to find it. What we think of ourselves or what we've done or haven't done with our lives can't stop us from finding peace. Freedom, joy, and life are waiting for anyone who genuinely desires to find it and has the courage to do something about it.

Do you have the courage?

THANKS

Thank you Hiranya for all your love, support and companionship. You are my best friend.

Thank you to Maharishi Krishnananda for all your time, commitment and love. You had faith in me when I didn´t.

Thanks Priya and Hiranya for the brilliant book cover.

Thank you to Meera and Caroline for great editing.

Thanks Chandan for the catchy book title.

Thanks to my parents for their love and patience.

Thank you Lukas, for your kindness and passion.

Thanks also to Charlie, Garuda, Govinda, Paramananda, Devadatta, Sri, Suvarna, Shanti, Maharani, Narain, Matt, Mike, Jim and Rex.

ABOUT THE AUTHOR

Maitreya was a Sales Trader in a top investment bank in London. Stressed out, he quit the rat race and set out to find peace.
A few near death experiences later he stumbled across a mysterious group of monks who taught him a method to cultivate inner peace.

Maitreya, and the other Ishayas´of the Brightpath, now teach the simple and powerful method of finding peace. Maitreya also gives talks and workshops all over the world.

He lives in Oslo with his fiancé, his stepson and two bonsai trees.

If you would like to contact Maitreya, or book
him for talks or seminars take a look at:

www.thebrokerwhobrokefree.com

If you are interested in learning the
Ishayas´Ascension techniques take a look at:

www.thebrightpath.com

Printed in Great Britain
by Amazon.co.uk, Ltd.,
Marston Gate.